W9-BNI-558

Soccer File

PASSING

and

DRIBBLING

by James Nixon

Photography by Bobby Humphrey

A+

Smart Apple Media

Published by Smart Apple Media
P.O. Box 3263, Mankato, Minnesota 56002

Printed in the United States of America at Corporate
Graphics, in North Mankato, Minnesota.

Published by arrangement with the Watts Publishing
Group Ltd., London.

Library of Congress Cataloging-in-Publication Data
Nixon, James, 1982-
  Passing and dribbling / James Nixon; photography by
Bobby Humphrey.
    p. cm. -- (Soccer file)
  Includes index.
  ISBN 978-1-59920-528-1 (library binding)
 1. Passing (Soccer)--Juvenile literature. 2. Dribbling
(Soccer)--Juvenile literature. I. Title.
  GV943.9.P37N59 2012
  796.334'2--dc22

                                2010041756

Planning and production by
Discovery Books Limited
Editor: James Nixon
Design: Blink Media
Illustrations: Stefan Chabluk

The author, packager, and publisher
would like to thank the children of
Farsley Celtic Junior Football Club for
their participation in this book.

1020
2-2011

9 8 7 6 5 4 3 2 1

Photo acknowledgements:
Getty Images: pp. 5 top (Robert Mora/MLS), 17
bottom (Antonio Scorza/AFP); Istockphoto.com: pp.
4 bottom, 7 middle, 11 left; Shutterstock: pp. 4 top
(Sportsphotographer.eu), 6 top (Andreas Gradin),
13 bottom (Jonathan Larsen), 14 top (Andreas
Gradin), 18 right (Jonathan Larsen), 20 top (Andreas
Gradin), 23 bottom (Jonathan Larsen), 24 bottom
(Sportsphotographer.eu), 25 right (Sport Graphic), 27
top-right and 28 top (Jonathan Larsen), 28 bottom
(Laszio Szirtesi), 29 (Jonathan Larsen).

Cover photos: Shutterstock: left (Jonathan Larsen),
right (Andreas Gradin).

Every attempt has been made to clear copyright.
Should there be any inadvertent omission please
apply to the publisher
for rectification.

Statistics on pages 28–29 are correct at the time
of going to press, but in the fast-moving world of
soccer are subject to change.

Contents

Words that appear in **bold** are in the glossary on page 30.

The MIDFIELD Battle

Goals are vital and defending is key, but a soccer game is often won or lost in the midfield. Most of the game takes place in the middle of the field. If your midfielders are good at winning the ball and keeping possession, your team can control the game. You will stop the other team from building attacks and allow your midfield to create scoring chances for the forwards.

Midfielders look to pass or dribble as they build an attack.

When you win the ball in midfield or receive a pass, what should you do? The most important thing is to not give away possession of the ball. You have to act quickly as an opponent will soon challenge you. At the same time, you must think about advancing the ball forward. There are two main ways to do this. You can pass to a teammate or dribble with the ball.

When under pressure from opponents, you must battle to keep possession of the ball for your team.

EXPERT: XAVI

Spanish midfielder Xavi (right) is possibly the finest **playmaker** in the world. A playmaker directs the team's play from midfield. Most of Spain's passing and offensive moves go through Xavi. He has great vision and directs passes all over the field with accuracy. He rarely gives the ball away. A team with Xavi on it is likely to dominate a game. Xavi was named "Man of the Match" when his club Barcelona beat Manchester United 2–0 in the 2009 Champions League Final.

Ball Familiarity

Before you become an expert at passing and dribbling, you should learn how the ball responds to your touch. Practice getting a feel for the ball with these exercises. Make sure you practice using both feet. In a game, you cannot always use your stronger foot.

▸ Roll your foot over the top of the ball and down the side (below 1–3). Now keep going from one side to the other.
▸ Next, practice your feel for the ball on the move. Set up two cones a short distance apart, and dribble the ball around the cones in a figure eight.
▸ When you are more confident, try some ball juggling. How many times can you touch the ball in the air without it dropping (left)?

1

2

3

SHORT Passing

During a game, players use a variety of passes. A simple, sidefooted, short pass along the ground is very accurate and a good way to keep possession. The drawback is its lack of power.

Make sure the ball reaches its target and does not get intercepted.

Sidefoot pass

Sidefoot Pass

▸ Plant your non-kicking foot by the ball, and point it in the direction you want to pass.
▸ Swing your leg back, turning your foot outward.
▸ With your body over the ball, strike the middle of the ball firmly with the inside of your foot (left).
▸ Keep your ankle firm, and follow through smoothly and low.

Curling Pass

A sidefoot pass is the most common, but you can make passes with other parts of the foot. If a defender is in the way, you can curve the ball around them. To do this, you still use the inside of your foot, but higher up toward your laces (**instep**). Strike the ball just off-center, and follow through to curl it.

Instep

Outside Foot Pass

A simple pass with the outside of the shoe is to tap it with the area around your little toe. There is no backswing or follow-through. The power of the pass comes from a sideways flick of your ankle. It is a good pass to use when you are under pressure from a defender because it can be done quickly (left).

Tricky Passes

There are other more difficult passes you can use in a game.

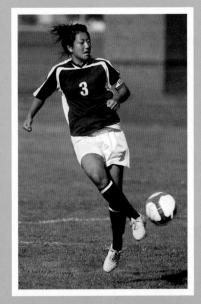

A back heel is used to pass the ball backward. When you kick back with the heel, you need to keep your foot level in the air for a clean contact (above).

When the ball is in the air, you can try a first-time header or volley-pass to a teammate. When volleying a short pass (above), keep your eye on the ball, your knee bent, and use the inside of your foot to steer it to the receiver.

A headed pass usually needs to be **cushioned**. This means pushing the ball forward gently so your pass will be accurate and not too hard. To control the header, your body should be relaxed with your knees bent.

LONG Passing

A long pass moves the ball upfield quickly. It is often used as an offensive pass to the forwards. It is harder to find the target with a long pass, and possession can be lost.

1

2

3

Weight of Pass

Kicking a pass with the right amount of power is just as important as accuracy. The receiver of the pass should be able to control your pass. It is no good to blast the ball. Equally, don't hit it too softly or a defender might intercept it.

Lofted Pass

The longest passes have to be **lofted**. If you hit the ball along the ground, it might be intercepted by an opponent. This is how you loft a pass:

▶ Approach the ball at a slight angle, and plant your non-kicking leg beside the ball.
▶ Swing your leg back, and lean your body back slightly (1).
▶ Strike the lower half of the ball so that the bottom of your instep slides under it (2).
▶ Make sure you have a long, smooth follow-through (3).

The Drive Pass

If you want to send a long pass along the ground, the best method is to drive it with your instep. This will keep it low, but also give you power.

▸ Your shoe laces should make contact with the middle of the ball (left).
▸ Keep your toes down and your heel up.
▸ Get your knee over the ball to keep it low, and have your arms spread for balance.

Swerve It

You can swerve the drive pass by cutting across the ball and striking it with the outside of your instep (1). Your follow-through should sweep across your body (2).

PRACTICE DRILL:

Pass Through the Gate

Practice a variety of long passes with a friend. Each should stand between a pair of cones some distance away from each other. Try to aim lofted passes and drive passes through the cones.

BALL Control

Controlling a pass you receive from a teammate is one of the most important skills in soccer. Most of the time, you will want the ball under control before you can dribble, pass, or shoot. Everything depends on your first touch.

First Touch

A poor first touch fails to get the ball under control. If the ball bounces away, an opponent could take possession. Your first touch should do two things:

▸ It should protect the ball from challenging players.
▸ It should set you up for your next move.

Cushioning

A good first touch stops the ball just in front of your feet. To do this, you have to cushion the ball to take the speed out of it.

▸ Position your foot in line with the flight of the ball (1).
▸ On contact, relax your foot, and draw it back with the ball. This slows the ball down and gets it under control (2).
▸ An alternative is to trap the ball under the sole of your foot. Do this slightly in front of you so the ball is in a position to be kicked afterward (3).

Tips

▶ Before the ball reaches you, take a quick look around, and plan your next move.

▶ Your first touch doesn't have to be cushioned: you can nudge the ball in the direction you want to go. This is useful if you can see a space to move into (above right).

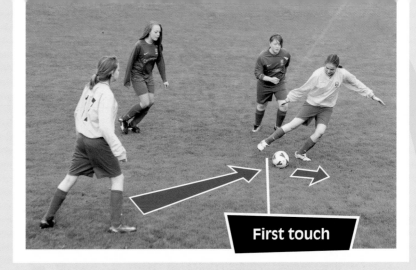

First touch

▶ Help your teammates by calling to them as they receive the ball. Two common calls are: "Turn"—tells the player they have space to turn on the ball and face the other way. "Man on"—tells the player they are under pressure from an opponent.

Control in the Air

You can control the ball with almost any part of your body.

Instep—This is used to control the ball in the air. Bend your knee, and lower your leg on impact to cushion the ball.

Thigh—Control a high ball on the thigh by lifting your leg off the ground. Keep your arms spread out wide for balance.

Chest—Cushion the ball on the chest by leaning back slightly and letting the ball fall to your feet.

TEAMWORK

To keep possession and build an offense, you need good passing, but also good teamwork. When a teammate has the ball, you should support them and be ready to receive a pass. The movement of players off the ball is vital to a team's success.

Finding Space

Pass and Move

When you make a pass, don't stand and admire it. Get moving right away to support the player you have just passed to. Quick passing and moving can destroy a team's defense.

When your team is in possession, you need to be constantly on the move, looking for spaces where a teammate can pass to you. Shout to your teammate, and call for the ball (above). Even if the ball is not passed to you, you will have lured a defender away from the play. This is called a **decoy run** (below).

Decoy run

One-Two Pass

This pass and move technique is just as good as dribbling around an opponent. Pass the ball to a teammate, and sprint off to collect the return pass.

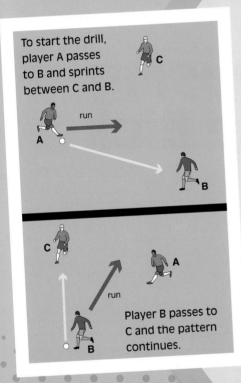

To start the drill, player A passes to B and sprints between C and B.

run

A

B

C

C

run

A

Player B passes to C and the pattern continues.

B

PRACTICE DRILL:
Moving Triangles

This drill trains you not to stand and watch your passes. Set three players up in a triangle (left) and pass and move as instructed below to move your triangle up the field.

▶ Player A passes to B and sprints between B and C.
▶ Player B controls the ball, passes to C, and sprints between A and C.
▶ Player C passes to A, sprints between A and B, and this pattern continues.
▶ Race against another triangle of players and see whose team can move up the field the quickest.

EXPERT: Michael Bradley

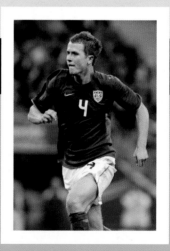

Midfielder Michael Bradley is a rising star in the United States soccer team. His all-around passing game is excellent. Like all good passers of the ball, he is always on the lookout for that offensive pass that could create a scoring chance for a teammate.

PICKING Your Pass

A good pass is not just about technique and accuracy, but also about choosing the right pass. The best pass to use depends on the situation. So, how do you decide whom to pass to and when?

Choosing Your Kick

Look around you and see who is in a position to receive the ball. A player in an open space is generally the best option. Make sure there is a clear route for your pass. Low passes are more accurate, but if defenders are in the way, use a high pass to clear their heads.

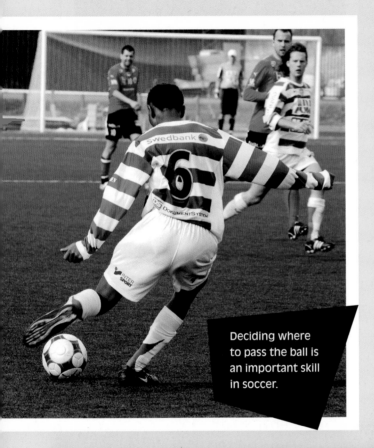

Deciding where to pass the ball is an important skill in soccer.

Drawing the Player

The best time to play a pass is the moment before a defender challenges you. Drawing the player in creates space in front of you to pass. A teammate can run down the side of you to receive the pass. This is called an **overlapping run**. If your teammate is running forward into space, pass the ball in front of them. Passing to his or her feet will slow them down.

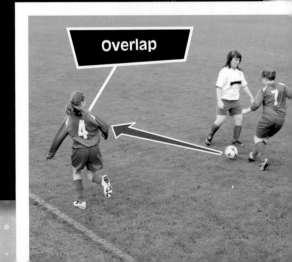

Overlap

A Risk Worth Taking?

A forward pass is better for the team than a backward pass. However, you may risk losing the ball by forward passing. If in doubt, play a simple sideways or backward pass to keep possession. On the other hand, playing back when a forward pass is possible is a poor decision. It is a wasted opportunity for the team. You have to learn when to play a safe pass, and when to use a more risky offensive pass.

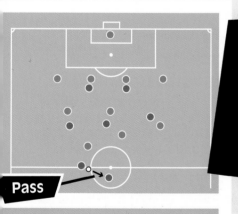

Pass

Here, a short sideways pass is the best option to keep possession. Be patient, and wait for a better opening.

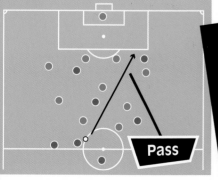

Pass

In this situation, space has opened up for an offensive pass. Look for a forward pass whenever you can.

Disguise

Don't always choose the obvious pass. Try to surprise the defender. You can trick the defender by looking away from your target and changing the angle of your foot at the last moment (below).

Instant Pass

A first-time pass without controlling the ball is harder to make. But it is a good pass to use if you are about to be challenged. It also makes your team's offense quicker and harder to defend against.

The KILLER Pass

A team's passing move will hopefully end up with a "final ball." A final ball is that killer pass that leads to a scoring opportunity.

Through Balls

The closer you are to an opponent's goal, the more crowded the space becomes. It takes great skill to find a forward with your pass and set up a chance for a goal. One of the best offensive passes is the through ball. Here, you have to thread your pass through the defensive line for the forward to run on to. The timing of the pass is crucial. It has to be played the moment your teammate takes off to run. If you're too late, the forward will be **offside**.

Through ball

Crossing

Another important offensive pass is the **cross**. This is a long pass to forwards in the box from out wide near the **sideline**. When hit with speed and accuracy, a cross can be devastating to a defense.

Crossing Tips

- Use the instep-drive pass or bend it with the inside of your instep to get speed on the cross.
- Look up before you cross to check the position of your teammates in the box.
- Try to get your cross in as early as possible, so the defenders are caught off-guard.
- If you are near the **byline**, curl your cross away from the goaltender so they can't catch it (right).

EXPERT: Kaká

Brazilian playmaker Kaká is one of the superstars of the game. In 2009, Real Madrid bought Kaká from AC Milan for a massive $94 million. Kaká is famous for the number of **assists** he achieves. An assist is a move that sets up a goal. He is great at spotting an opening for a through pass. His timing of the pass and the weight he puts on the ball are judged to perfection, so the forward can run to the ball and score.

SHIELDING and Turning

You may find yourself in a tight spot, under pressure, with no time or room to make a pass. Now is the time to shield, or screen, the ball.

Shielding is a great way to hold on to the ball and stop your opponents from stealing possession.

How to Shield

1

2

3

- As soon as you receive the ball, put your body between the ball and your opponent. Stepping over the ball is a simple way of doing this. The ball is now protected. The defender cannot reach it (1).
- You now have more time to choose your pass. A backward pass is fine if no other pass is possible.
- Hold your arms out and keep your knees bent as your shield.
- Be strong in holding your ground. It is okay to use your body to hold off your opponent, as long as you don't push.
- Turn yourself at a slight angle to the ball so you can keep an eye on the opponent behind you (2).
- While shielding, you can roll the ball from side to side with the sole of your foot to stop the defender from taking it (3).

The Spin-Off

From the shielding position, your next step might be a pass. But you can also try spinning away from your opponent with good close control and a quick change of speed. You can turn in a circle either way using the outside or the inside of your foot. Swivel on your standing foot (1), bring your other foot over, and tap the ball two or three times to circle around your opponent (2). With your last touch of the turn, accelerate away from the defender (3).

1

2

3

PRACTICE DRILL:
Keep the Ball

With a partner, see who can shield the ball from the other for the longest. The player shielding the ball must try to keep the ball in the circle.

Basic DRIBBLING

Passing is one way to get the ball up the field. The other is dribbling. Soccer players who can run with the ball around defenders, with the ball almost stuck to their feet, are some of the most exciting players to watch.

Dribbling is risky business. Defenders will soon try to tackle you. Only the most skillful players in the game can dribble for long without losing the ball.

Moving with the Ball

If you are on the ball and have space in front of you, now is a good time to dribble. Run forward, kicking the ball with sharp taps to keep it close in front of you.

▸ You can dribble with the inside or outside of either foot, but try not to tap the ball too far out to the side (1).

▸ You can dribble more quickly using the outside of your foot (2).

▸ Don't let the ball get stuck under your feet. It will slow you down.

▸ Don't kick the ball too far forward. You will lose control and possession of the ball.

▸ Switch between looking up and looking down when you dribble, so you can see where your teammates and opponents are (3).

PRACTICE DRILL:
Kick It Out

This game teaches you to be aware of your surroundings while you dribble. Players dribble around the inside of a circle. You must be on the move at all times, trying to keep control of your ball. At the same time, you must try to kick other players' balls out of the circle. Whoever has their ball kicked out the least wins.

PRACTICE DRILL:
Slalom

Set up a slalom course with cones and dribble as closely around them as possible. Practice kicking the ball with both feet as you dribble, and increase your speed as you improve. The zigzagging will improve your balance on the ball, which is vital for dribbling.

CHANGING Pace and Direction

Once you have mastered the basics of moving with the ball, you are ready to try to dribble around defenders. Defenders will do everything they can to stop you. You will need some kind of trick to get past them.

Change of Pace

- The best way to throw your opponent off is a sudden change of pace.
- As you approach your opponent, slow down.
- Watch for the chance to dodge past your opponent with a quick change of speed. As you go past them, continue to accelerate.

Changing Direction

Many of the game's greatest dribblers have lots of speed. But you don't have to be super-fast to be a top dribbler. Defenders are just as easily fooled by skillful ball control. Quick changes of direction can leave defenders far behind.

Feinting

Feinting means pretending to dribble past your opponent in one direction, but actually moving the other way. This is how you do it:

- Facing your opponent, drop your shoulder and lean as though you are going to move around one side of them (1).
- As the defender moves to block you, swerve your body back the other way (2).
- Accelerate past your opponent with the ball before they have time to recover.

Stepovers

Players often choose to step over the ball as they feint. This is a flick with the outside of the foot in the direction you are pretending to move. Instead of touching the ball, circle your foot around it (1). Then, you can move off in the other direction (2). Putting a series of **stepovers** together, from one foot to the other, can really confuse a defender!

Fake Shot

Another good feint in soccer is the fake shot. Swing your leg back as if you are going to shoot. Instead, hook the ball with the inside of your foot and dart past the defender. The defender, who has moved to block the shot, will be off balance and completely fooled (left).

EXPERT: Frank Ribéry

Frenchman Frank Ribéry is one of the trickiest dribblers in world soccer. Ribéry attacks defenders with speed, energy, and skill. He is the master of quick and sharp changes of direction. He can hook the ball with the inside or the outside of his foot to fool defenders. Former World Player of the Year, Zinedine Zidane has described Ribéry as the "jewel of French soccer."

TRICK Turns

Basic changes of direction are good when you are running at defenders. In tighter situations, where you are being closely marked, you may need a more complicated skill to fool your opponent.

Drag Back

The drag back or "V move" is a great trick to use just as your **marker** puts their foot in to tackle. Drag the ball back with the sole of your foot (1), and, in the same movement, flick it forward past the defender. You can flick it with the outside of your foot one way (2) or with the inside of your foot and behind your standing leg the other way.

Cruyff Turn

The Cruyff turn is a very famous skill named after Dutch legend Johan Cruyff, who perfected the trick in the 1970s. Use it to turn away from a defender who is **jockeying** you.

▸ Shape your body as if you are going to pass or cross the ball.
▸ Instead, lean back and hook the ball with the inside of your foot and drag it behind your standing leg (right).
▸ Turn quickly, and follow the ball.

To do the Cruyff turn, hook the ball back behind your standing leg.

Stop Turn

1

2

3

If you are running with the ball, but you are being **closed down** (1), a stop turn is a good way to find more space. With this trick, stop the ball completely with the sole of your foot (2 and 3). Then, make a complete change of direction to go the opposite way. As you stop the ball, step over it, face the other way, and move away all in one quick movement (4).

EXPERT: Lionel Messi

Lionel Messi from Argentina is considered by many to be the most skillful player in the world. He has all the tricks in the book. Messi is very short for a soccer player, but he has such quick feet that he can outwit his larger and stronger opponents.

4

Dummy Turn

To get the better of defenders, you need to do the unexpected. **Dummies** are a great way to fool an opponent. A dummy is to pretend to do something. A dummy turn is a good way to lose your marker. Step over the ball, and lean as if you were going to turn in the other direction. Then, shift your weight back the other way to keep going straight.

FANCY Tricks

There are some spectacular tricks you can try to pull off to beat your opponent. But be warned: these are very difficult and very risky to try in a game. Only the top players try these moves in a game.

360-Spin Move

With this trick, you do a full turn of your body, taking the ball with you past the defender. It feels like you are walking on the ball.

▶ As you approach your opponent while dribbling, put your foot on top of the ball, and start to turn your body (1).

▶ Roll the ball back toward your other foot, and continue turning your body (2 and 3).

▶ Drag the ball past your opponent with the sole of the foot, finish turning your body to face the ball, and run away with it (4 and 5).

Flick-Up

This trick lifts the ball over the opponent for you to run toward.

▸ Trap the ball between the toes of your back foot and heel of your front foot.
▸ Roll the ball up the heel and flick it high into the air.
▸ To make sure the ball moves forward in the air, lean forward slightly as you do this trick (above).

EXPERT: Marta

Brazilian Marta Viera da Silva, better known simply as Marta, is without doubt the most skillful player in women's soccer. Her supreme dribbling skills are what make her so dangerous to defenders. She often uses the 360-spin move. Marta is the only player to win the FIFA Women's World Player of the Year five times in a row.

Nutmegs

A good way to dribble past a defender is to put the ball through his or her legs. This is called a nutmeg. Defenders will keep their legs close together to stop you from doing this. Here is a skill to give you the chance at a nutmeg.

▸ Pretend to kick the ball past the opponent, but step over it instead.
▸ As the defender goes to block this dummy kick, flick the ball through their legs with the inside of your other foot (right).

MIDFIELD Stars

Here is a selection of some of the finest passers and dribblers in the world today. These players are capable of running the show from midfield.

Each profile looks at the trophies the players have won individually and as part of a team.

Cesc Fabregas

D.O.B: 5.4.87
Nation: Spain
Height: 5'9" (1.75 m)
Weight: 152 lbs (69 kg)
International Caps (Goals) 56 (6)

Club record:	Appearances	(Goals)
2003– Arsenal	279	(53)

Honors: FA Cup 2005; European Championship 2008; FIFA World Cup 2010
Top Award:
Named in PFA Team of the Year 2009–10

Kaká

D.O.B: 4.22.82   **Nation:** Brazil
Height: 6'1" (1.86 m)   **Weight:** 161 lbs (73 kg)
International Caps (Goals) 82 (27)

Club record:	Appearances	(Goals)
2001–2003 Sao Paulo	75	(30)
2003–2009 AC Milan	270	(95)
2009– Real Madrid	33	(9)

Honors: Italian League 2004; Champions League 2007; FIFA Club World Cup 2008; FIFA World Cup 2002
Top Award:
World Player of the Year 2007

Lionel Messi

D.O.B: 6.24.87   **Nation:** Argentina
Height: 5'6" (1.69 m)   **Weight:** 148 lbs (67 kg)
International Caps (Goals) 52 (14)

Club record:	Appearances	(Goals)
2005– Barcelona	230	(146)

Honors: Spanish League 2005, 2006, 2009; Spanish Cup 2009; Champions League 2006, 2009; Olympics 2008
Top Award:
World Soccer Young Player of the Year 2008

Steven Gerrard

D.O.B: 5.30.80
Nation: England
Height: 6 ft. (1.83 m)
Weight: 183 lbs (83 kg)
International Caps (Goals) 88 (19)

Club record:	Appearances	(Goals)
1999– Liverpool	544	(139)

Honors: FA Cup 2001, 2006; UEFA Champions League 2005; UEFA Cup 2001
Top Award:
Soccer Player of the Year 2009 (England)

Michael Bradley

D.O.B: 7.31.87
Nation: United States
Height: 6'2" (1.88 m)
Weight: 165 lbs (75 kg)
International Caps (Goals) 50 (8)

Club record:	Appearances	(Goals)
2004–2005 Metrostars	31	(1)
2005–2008 Heerenveen	57	(20)
2008– Borussia Monchengladbach	68	(9)

Honors: CONCACAF Gold Cup 2007
Top Award:
U.S. Soccer Young Athlete of the Year 2007

Robinho

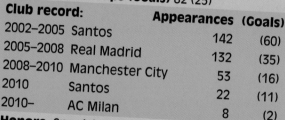

D.O.B: 1.25.84
Nation: Brazil
Height: 5'9" (1.75 m)
Weight: 132 lbs (60 kg)
International Caps (Goals) 82 (25)

Club record:		Appearances	(Goals)
2002–2005	Santos	142	(60)
2005–2008	Real Madrid	132	(35)
2008–2010	Manchester City	53	(16)
2010	Santos	22	(11)
2010–	AC Milan	8	(2)

Honors: Spanish League 2007, 2008;
Copa America 2007
Top Award:
World Soccer Young Player of the Year 2005

Marta

D.O.B: 2.19.86
Nation: Brazil
Height: 5'½" (1.54 m)
Weight: 126 lbs (57 kg)
International Caps (Goals) 54 (54)

Club record:	Appearances	(Goals)
2004–2008 Umea IK	103	(111)
2009–2010 Los Angeles Sol	19	(10)
2009–2010 Santos	14	(26)
2010 FC Gold Pride	24	(19)
2011– Western New York Flash		

Honors: Swedish League 2005, 2006, 2007, 2008; Swedish Cup 2007
Top Award:
Women's Professional Soccer MVP 2009, 2010

Frank Ribéry

D.O.B: 4.7.83   **Nation:** France
Height: 5'7" (1.70 m)   **Weight:** 159 lbs (72 kg)
International Caps (Goals) 48 (7)

Club record:		Appearances	(Goals)
2004–2005	Metz	22	(1)
2005	Galatasaray	17	(1)
2005–2007	Marseille	91	(19)
2007–	Bayern Munich	116	(42)

Honors: Turkish Cup 2005; German Cup 2008;
German League 2008; FIFA World Cup 2002
Top Award:
Footballer of the Year 2008 (Germany)

Statistics in this book are correct at the time of going to press, but in the fast-moving world of soccer are subject to change.

29

Glossary

assist a pass from which a teammate scores

byline the line at each end of the field to either side of the goal

closed down surrounded by one or more defenders

cross a long pass from the side of the field into the penalty box

cushion soften the impact of the ball to control it

decoy run a movement by an offender that leads a defender away from where the ball will actually go

dummy a pretend turn, pass, or kick

feinting pretending to make an offensive move

instep the part of the foot where your shoelaces are

intercept to stop an opponent's pass from reaching its intended destination

jockeying stopping opponents on the ball from moving forward by staying at their feet and blocking their movement

loft to kick the ball high into the air

marker a defender who stays close to an opponent

offside a position on the field where the ball cannot be passed to you; to be onside, you must have two opponents between you and the opponents' goal.

off the ball when a player does not have possession of the ball

overlapping run a run from behind and down the side of a teammate on the ball to provide support

playmaker a player who leads the offense and sets up goalscoring chances for the strikers

possession when you or your teammate has control of the ball

sideline the boundary line on each side of the field

stepover a sharp movement of the leg over the ball instead of kicking it to fool a defender

Further Information

Books

Soccer: The Ultimate Guide by Martin Cloake (DK Pub, 2010)

The Soccer Book: The Sport, the Teams, the Tactics, the Cups by Johnny Acton and David Goldblatt (DK Pub, 2009)

Soccer Players and Skills by Clive Gifford (PowerKids Press, 2011)

Soccer Step-by-Step by Madeleine Jennings and Ian Howe (Rosen Central, 2010)

Web Sites

http://www.expertfootball.com/training/techniques.php
Get advice on skills to use in your games.

http://www.soccer-training-info.com/soccer_move_videos.asp
Watch videos of the pros doing moves such as the nutmeg and the step over.

http://www.marta10.com/en/
Get news and facts, and view pictures and videos of Marta, 5 times FIFA Women's World Player of the Year.

http://www.soccerxpert.com
Improve your soccer skills with these tips and drills.

Note to parents and teachers: Every effort has been made by the publishers to ensure that these web sites are suitable for children, that they are of the highest educational value, and that they contain no inappropriate or offensive material. However, because of the nature of the Internet, it is impossible to guarantee that the contents of these sites will not be altered. We strongly advise that Internet access is supervised by a responsible adult.

Index